A chickaDEE Book

© 2008 Bayard Canada Books Inc.

Publisher: Jennifer Canham
Editorial Director: Mary Beth Leatherdale
Creative Director: Barb Kelly
Editor: Katherine Dearlove
Production Coordinator: Paul Markowski
Production Editor: Larissa Byj
Production Assistant: Kathy Ko
Cover and Design Concepts: Claudia Dávila
Layout: Stephanie Olive

Comics by Jay Stephens and Steven Charles Manale

Thanks to Hilary Bain, Wendy Ding,
Angela Keenlyside, Melissa Owens,
Susan Sinclair, and Aron Slipacoff.

We gratefully acknowledge the financial support of the Government of Canada through the Book Publishing Industry Development Program (BPIDP) for our publishing activities.

 Conseil des Arts   Canada Council
du Canada   for the Arts

Library and Archives Canada Cataloguing in Publication

    You Crack Me Up! : Chick and Dee's Big Book of Fun /
[Illustrators, Steven Charles Manale, Jay Stephens].

  (You Crack Me Up Series ; #1)
A chickaDEE book.
ISBN 978-2-89579-191-1

    1. Puzzles--Juvenile literature. 2. Wit and humor--Juvenile literature.
3. Chick (Fictitious character). 4. Dee (Fictitious character).
I. Manale, Steven Charles, 1972- II. Stephens, Jay, 1971- III. Series.

GV1493.Y67 2008   J793.73   C2007-907077-9

Printed and bound in Canada

Owlkids Publishing
10 Lower Spadina Ave., Suite 400
Toronto, ON M5V 2Z2
Ph: 416-340-2700
Fax: 416-340-9769

Publisher of

ChiRP   chickaDEE   OWL

www.owlkids.com

You Crack Me Up! #1

Chick and Dee's Big Book of Fun

Jay Stephens and
Steven Charles Manale

Owl kids

Contents

Comics

Meet the Gang!
Page 61

Puzzles and Fun

Flip the corners to see an animated flipbook. Page 17

Bonus

Arf's Funnies
Tons of Jokes!

BRUNO   ROBIN   PETAL   ARF

Introducing

Chick and Dee

LUNCH CRUNCH

MUSEUM MIX-UP

Spot the Differences

Gang's

Can you spot 10 differences between these two pictures?

All Here!

Answers page 79

21

Spot the Differences
Fishing

Can you spot 10 differences between these two pictures?

Answers page 79

Did You Know?

Chick and Dee share some of the gang's secrets.

Find out **even more** about Chick, Dee, and their pals on page 61.

HOW DID CHICK AND DEE MEET?

KLONK!

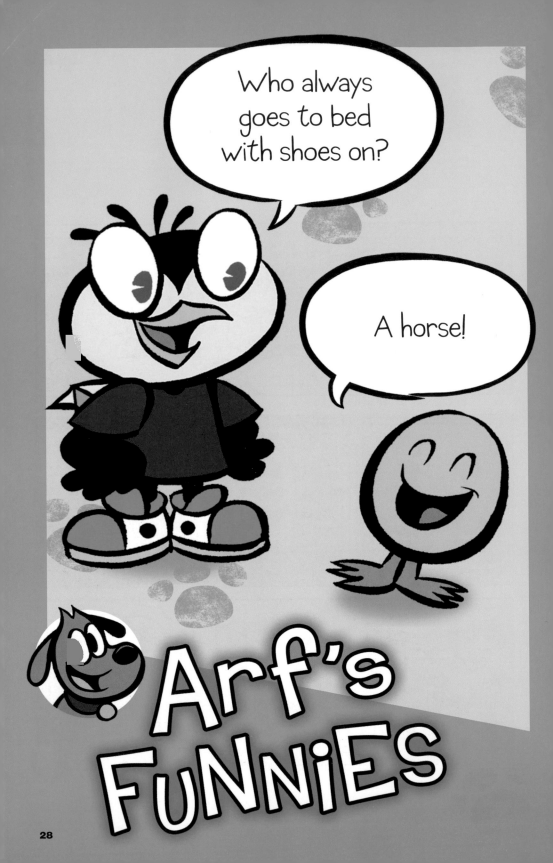

What is green and red all over?
A pickle holding its breath!
Arf's FuNNiES

THE SLEEPOVER

SHELLDON'S HERO

Give **food** to a food bank.

Cheer Up a sad friend by making a funny drawing.

YOU can be a

Pick Up Litter on your way home from school.

RECYCLING

Read a story
to a younger kid.

Hero Every Day!

Surprise
your parents and do an extra chore.

Help an older person cross the road.

Which character are YOU most like?

1 **What is your favourite sport?**

   a. Hockey
   b. Soccer
   c. Pogo-sticking
   d. Bowling

2 **Which snack would you choose?**

   a. Choco-berry swirl pudding
   b. Skyscraper sandwich
   c. Banana ice cream
   d. Tuna sandwiches

3 What would you take on vacation?

a. A backpack stuffed to the top
b. Bags of snacks
c. Your favourite pranks
d. Your super-cool sunglasses

4 What is your perfect pet?

a. Colourful fish
b. Playful puppy
c. Cuddly guinea pig
d. Fast horse

5 What do you like to do on weekends?

a. Play in your tree house
b. Have a sleepover
c. Read a book
d. Go to the movies

6 What's your favourite game?

a. Four square
b. Crazy eights
c. Hopscotch
d. Hide-and-seek

RESULTS

Count how many of each letter you circled.

Mostly A's: Chick

Mostly B's: Dee

Mostly C's: Petal

Mostly D's: Shelldon

THE SCARE

HOT GOALIE

All-star

Can you spot 10 differences between these two pictures?

Heroes!

Answers page 79

ARF'S DAY

KING OF KARATE

THE BIG SALE

Read
library books.

Take a
Litterless
Lunch.

7 Easy ways YOU can

No Flyers
Please!

Make a sign
for your mailbox.

Make crafts
out of used things.

make every day Earth Day!

Ride
your
bike.

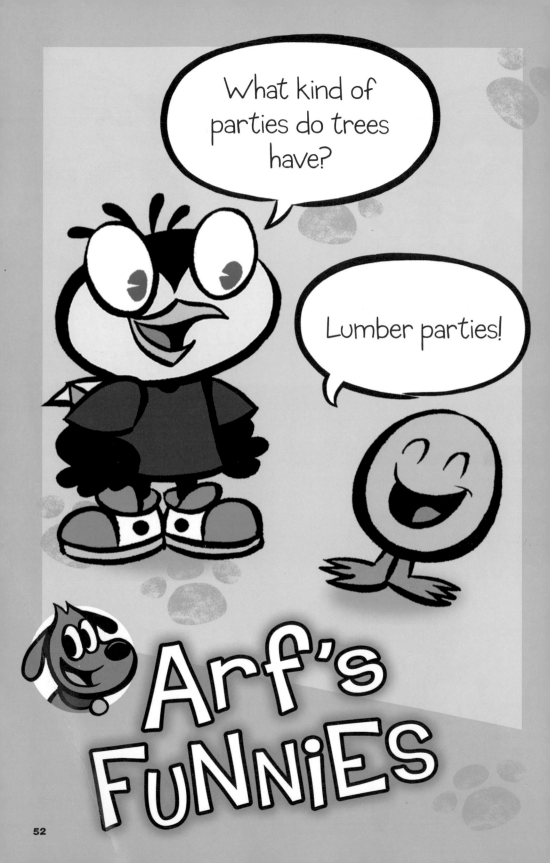

Comic SPECIAL
TROUBLE IN THE TREE HOUSE

Puzzling Patterns

Get from the start of this maze to the finish by following the directions below. The first step is done for you.

Meet the Gang!

Meet the Gang

Get the scoop on Chick and Dee and all their friends.

This is Chick! He is Dee's best pal. Chick loves sports, especially hockey and soccer. When he's not playing, Chick dreams about building. The gang was happy when he thought up plans for a new tree house.

Did you know? Chick does three jumping jacks before bed.

Meet Dee! He is Chick's best pal. He loves to eat, snack, and munch. In fact, he's hungry right now! Dee loves a good laugh, especially with his little brother Shelldon.

Did you know? Dee adds chocolate syrup to his skyscraper sandwiches.

SHELLDON

Shelldon is Dee's little brother. He doesn't say much, but boy is he smart. And he's super strong, too. You should see him do karate!

Did you know? Shelldon wants to be a movie star when he grows up.

HA!

FANG

Fang the alligator is a bully. At least he tries to be. With his pal Jack, Fang comes up with ideas to trick Chick and Dee. Luckily, his ideas never work.

Did you know? Fang likes to knit striped socks.

JACK

Jack the bat is the other bully. He follows Fang around, but deep down he's no meanie. When he's at home, Jack snacks on sardine pizza and reads comics.

Did you know? Jack sings lullabies in the shower.

BRUNO

Bruno might be a monster, but he is the friendliest monster around. Bruno loves to paint and draw pictures for his friends. Bruno loves riding his bike, and he gives the best piggybacks ever!

Did you know? Bruno is afraid of bunnies.

ROBIN

Chick's big sister Robin is like a big sister to everyone. She likes to cook but usually ends up making a mess. Maybe it's because she dances while she bakes.

Did you know? Robin doesn't like the colour pink.

PETAL

Petal likes to play pranks on the gang. She doesn't even mind when the joke's on her. Her favourite snacks are banana-bug swirl ice cream and spider sandwiches.

Did you know? Petal can read four chapter books in a week.

ARF

Ruff! Arf is the neighbourhood dog. He has lots of doggie friends. When his best pals are in school, Arf dances and watches scary movies. He also loves to catch a Frisbee.

Did you know? Arf secretly likes cats.

Learn to Draw!

Grab a pencil and paper!
Follow the step-by-step
instructions to draw Chick,
Dee, and friends.

Draw Chick

1

- Draw a big oval for Chick's head and a diamond for his beak.
- Make a triangle body.

2

- Add two more ovals for his eyes. Make the ovals slightly tilted.

3

- For legs, draw two lines under the triangle.
- Add two triangles on the sides for sleeves.

4

- Make small ovals for Chick's pupils.
- Add rectangles for arms.
- Add two half-circles for shoes (be sure to add the soles!).

5

- Draw two triangles in Chick's pupils.
- Add feathers and a black outline around his face.
- Make four ovals on each arm for fingers.

6

- Erase all the overlapping lines and trace Chick's outline with a black marker.
- Then colour him in.

You just drew Chick!

Draw Dee

1

- Make a big circle for Dee's head.
- Make a triangle body.
- Draw a half-circle at the bottom of the triangle.

2

- Add an oval in the middle of the big circle for an eye.
- Draw two long triangles for arms and two short triangles for legs.

3

- Draw another oval for the other eye.
- Make small ovals for pupils.
- Make two ovals for Dee's feet.

4

- Draw a curved line around the large ovals for Dee's goggles.
- Make four ovals on each arm for fingers.

5

6

- Make a rectangle for the goggle strap.
- Draw two curved triangles for Dee's mouth.
- Draw a jagged line for the bottom part of his shell.
- Add jagged lines for toes.

- Make a "D" on his shirt.
- Erase all the overlapping lines and trace Dee's outline with a black marker.
- Then colour him in.

You just drew Dee!

 # Draw Arf

1

• Draw two ovals for Arf's head and one for his body.

2

• Next, draw circles and ovals for Arf's legs.

3

• Draw a circle for Arf's nose.
• Then draw two ovals for Arf's eyes.
• Draw smaller ovals inside the eyes for pupils.

4

• Add Arf's ears and mouth.

5

- Add Arf's collar and tail. Then draw two triangles on Arf's head for fur.

6

- Erase the overlapping lines and trace Arf's outline with a black marker.
- Then colour him in.

You just drew Arf!

 # Draw Shelldon

1 2 3

- Draw an oval.
- Make it a little bit skinny at the top and fat at the bottom.

- Add eyes and mouth.
- Shelldon's eyes are just above the middle of his face.
- His mouth is a half-circle.

- Add legs and feet.
- Draw three points on each foot.
- Erase all overlapping lines and trace Shelldon's outline with a black marker.
- Then colour him in.

You just drew Shelldon!

Dress Shelldon up in different hats!

74

Drawing Tips

Change the look of your characters
by following these tips.

Put Chick and Dee
in different poses.

Change the shape of the characters' eyes
and mouths to change their moods.

Surprised

Sad

Scared

Happy

Meet the Illustrators

Jay Stephens

Jay Stephens created the popular "Chick and Dee" comic for *chickaDEE Magazine* in 1999. In 2002, he was nominated for a National Cartoonists Society Reuben Award in Magazine Illustration for his work on the comic. In 2004, Jay designed and co-illustrated the best-selling chickaDEE *Eat it Up!* cookbook for kids, written by his wife Elisabeth de Mariaffi, and featuring the cast from the "Chick and Dee" comics.

Jay is also the creator of the kids' comic strip *Welcome To... Oddville!*, the Emmy Award–winning animated series *Tutenstein and The Secret Saturdays*, and the author of the how-to-draw books *HEROES! Draw your Own Superheroes, Gadget Geeks and Other Do-Gooders; MONSTERS! Draw your Own Mutants, Freaks and Creeps;* and *ROBOTS! Draw your own Androids, Cyborgs and Battle Bots.*

Steven Charles Manale

Steven Charles Manale began writing and drawing the "Chick and Dee" comic in 2003. After attending the Ontario College of Art and Design, Steve worked briefly at an advertising agency. When he's not singing in his band, exhibiting in art shows, or doing commercial voice-overs, Steve is busy drawing things like dinosaurs, robots, stones, crowds, and giant skunks for the Toronto Raptors, YTV, and Thomson Nelson. Steve's webcomic *Superslackers* has been nominated for both the Ignatz and Joe Shuster awards.

Answers

Gang's All Here, page 14

Fishing for Fun, page 22

All-star Heroes, page 42

Puzzling Patterns, page 59

If you liked *You Crack Me Up!*, you'll love chickaDEE magazine

...the award-winning magazine created especially for kids (ages 6 to 9)

Ten times a year, *chickaDEE* subscribers get a fun mix of Chick and Dee comics, jokes, puzzles, animal facts, crafts, and easy science experiments that will entertain them while they build problem-solving skills and develop new ways of thinking.

All the fun and learning that you loved in *You Crack Me Up!* delivered to your door in *chickaDEE!*

Subscribe today at
www.owlkids.com/crackmeup
or call 1-800-551-6957